DIG SAFE

Also by Stuart Dischell

Evenings & Avenues
Good Hope Road
Animate Earth

Stuart Dischell

DIG
SAFE

 PENGUIN POETS

PENGUIN BOOKS

Published by the Penguin Group
Penguin Putnam Inc., 375 Hudson Street,
New York, New York 10014, U.S.A.
Penguin Books Ltd, 80 Strand,
London WC2R 0RL, England
Penguin Books Australia Ltd, 250 Camberwell Road, Camberwell,
Victoria 3124, Australia
Penguin Books Canada Ltd, 10 Alcorn Avenue,
Toronto, Ontario, Canada M4V 3B2
Penguin Books India (P) Ltd, 11 Community Centre, Panchsheel Park,
New Delhi—110 017, India
Penguin Books (N.Z.) Ltd, Cnr Rosedale and Airborne Roads, Albany,
Auckland, New Zealand
Penguin Books (South Africa) (Pty) Ltd, 24 Sturdee Avenue,
Rosebank, Johannesburg 2196, South Africa

Penguin Books Ltd, Registered Offices:
Harmondsworth, Middlesex, England

First published in Penguin Books 2003

1 2 3 4 5 6 7 8 9 10

LIBRARY OF CONGRESS CATALOGING-IN-PUBLICATION DATA
Dischell, Stuart
Dig Safe/Stuart Dischell.
p. cm.—(Penguin poets)
ISBN 0-14-200268-2
I. Title

PS3554.I827 D54 2003
811'.54—dc21
2002035480

Printed in the United States of America
Set in Janson Text
Designed by Francesca Belanger

for Mark and Adam

my brother and my son

ACKNOWLEDGMENTS

Certain of these poems, sometimes in different versions or under other titles, first appeared in these magazines and anthologies to which grateful acknowledgment is made:

Agni: ("Chorus of the Horses," "The Door," "The Hundred Pieces," and "A Mass Hallucination of Motels"); *Boston Book Review*: ("From the Anthology of Dreams of Death: Aerial Dream," "From the Anthology of Dreams of Death: Harlequin Dream," and "From the Anthology of Dreams of Death: Maritime Dream"); *Bostonia*: ("As I Dispose of an Old Encyclopedia" and "The Restaurant by the Pier"); *The Colorado Review*: ("Thin Song of the Leaky Faucet"); *88: A Journal of Contemporary Poetry*: ("Half Himself"); *The Gettysburg Review*: ("Flirt" and "A Traveler"); *Hayden's Ferry Review*: ("The Elevation" and "A Tenant at Will"); *The Kenyon Review*: ("Children of the City" and "The Lost City"); *Poems and Plays*: ("Poem for Jack"); *Poetry Miscellany*: ("The Landscape Artist" and "Neighbor to What Happens"); *Princeton University Library Chronicle*: ("The Puppet's Complaint"); *Slate*: ("Days of Me," "The Fisherman and the Dryad," "Prague," "The Report," and "Stevedore"); *The New Bread Loaf Anthology of Contemporary American Poetry*: ("Days of Me" and "A Fugitive Heart"); *Hammer and Blaze: A Gathering of Contemporary American Poets*: ("Crooked Wood" and "The Moth").

Have you ever wondered about those strange colored markings you sometimes find on the street or sidewalk? No, they're not a new kind of graffiti or modern art.

In fact, the markings represent underground utility lines. Yellow stands for gas or oil, red for electric, orange for telephone or cable television, blue for water and green for sewer lines. They've been painted on sidewalks as a safety measure to guide construction, utility or repair crews that may be digging in the area. These markings can also be considered as advertising for a program called Dig Safe.

—Fall River Gas Company

CONTENTS

DIG SAFE

Days of Me

When people say they miss me,
I think how much I miss me too,
Me, the old me, the great me,
Lover of three women in one day,
Modest me, the best me, friend
To waiters and bartenders, hearty
Laugher and name rememberer,
Proud me, handsome and hirsute
In soccer shoes and shorts
On the ball fields behind MIT,
Strong me in a weightbelt at the gym,
Mutual sweat dripper in and out
Of the sauna, furtive observer
Of the coeducated and scantily clad,
Speedy me, cyclist of rivers,
Goose and peregrine falcon
Counter, all season venturer,
Chatterer-up of corner cops,
Groundskeepers, mothers with strollers,
Outwitter of panhandlers and bill
Collectors, avoider of levies, excises,
Me in a taxi in the rain,
Pressing my luck all the way home.

That's me at the dice table, baby,
Betting come, little Joe, and yo,
Blowing the coals, laying thunder,
My foot on top a fifty dollar chip
Some drunk spilled on the floor,

Dishonest me, evener of scores,
Eager accepter of the extra change,
Hotel towel pilferer, coffee spoon
Lifter, fervent retailer of others'
Humor, blackhearted gossiper,
Poisoner at the well, dweller
In unsavory detail, delighted sayer
Of the vulgar, off course belier
Of the true me, empiric builder
Newly haircutted, stickerer-up
For pals, jam unpriser, medic
To the self-inflicted, attorney
To the self-indicted, petty accountant
And keeper of the double books,
Great divider of the universe
And all its forms of existence
Into its relationship to me,
Fellow trembler to the future,
Thin air gawker, apprehender
Of the frameless door.

The Report

Trying to remember what it was like to live
Here and how it was I used to feel and fit
Into those days—like a convict in the movies
I have come back to put on my old clothes.

Dogs I used to know give me a sniff.
The salt's on my skin; the air dark roasted.
Street people appear lucky and familiar.
I nod and some respond for whatever reason.

Better luck in shops where my kited checks
Clung to the register with a tail of tape—
In the stand of little birches set by itself
Where I kissed a neck in the bend of the river—

Behind windows where I looked out, life guard
To the street below, where my wife believed
Beautiful women passed just so I could see them,
Where my old cat, black bag of dust, blinked in the sun.

My memory is an upright sweeping back.
In its housing: coins and splinters, fingernails, fur,
Shells, grinds, and peels—the literal stuff of that bereft,
A man would be a scarecrow in a birdless field.

The Lost City

The lost city was not lost to itself.
Like rings, umbrellas, pens, or letters,
It stayed where it was; fogged in jungle,
Waiting to be touched like the furnishings
Of a blind man's home or the body of his wife
Naked beneath the blankets in a hotel room.

The lost city does not shiver or moan.
The stones of its alleys never miss the beat
Of its builders' hammers or the footfalls
Of the ones who called themselves citizens,
Who believed in generations, scratched emblems
Of fidelity upon their hearths and chiseled
Large above the columns of public structures;
Who were known for their music and dance,
Forms vacant as the torch fires in the chambers
That lit the scrawlings of what might have been
Holy places, grooved altars where the blood
Ran from the hearts of sacrificial beings.

The lost city awaits us with encrusted glitter
Like the ancestor's jewel we have never seen,
Buried with him in the grave of a hard country
To say, where the worms of his earth are serpents
Of the skull, where squirrels and dusty sparrows
Reside in his woods like jaguars and eagles.

Children of the City

I guess it was the rain that sent them
To her room, the urban rain that starts
With a great fuss but nothing like the rain
That catches you on a field or shore with no
Place to go. They might have stood in doorways,
Under awnings or parking lot overhangs,
By the edges of other peoples' umbrellas.
They might have gotten a drink or a cab
Or stepped inside the middle of a movie
When mystification makes all plots subtle,
The villain a hero of our own confusion,
Co-stars taking on the leading roles.
They might have indulged consumer desire,
Charging trench coats and festive rain hats,
Allowing themselves to be intimidated
By department store clerks, suited waiters,
Or couples who comment on the passing shoes.
They might have stood against a scrawny tree,
Pretending they had lost their forested way.
Instead, they agreed they did not like the rain,
That it bothered them and made them cold,
That they would follow the dotted puddles
Back where she would make them tea, where
They worried about their throats then kissed a lot
In the bathtub anyway. Leaning on the radiator,
Afterwards he wore her roommate's fuzzy robe.

A Fugitive Heart

She went to the bridge one weekend morning
Where the artists collected to sell their wares.
You've seen examples, mostly watercolors
Of Chartres, St. Paul's, or the Trevi Fountain.
Here and there a clown peers through greasepaint
Or a bouquet of asters has been drawn to scale.
Mostly, though, it's the architectural pictures
That sell their buyers the enduring pleasure,
An evidence of having been somewhere great
Or the good taste to have wanted to be there,
The true north of longing for the fugitive heart.
He was one of the artists, a young man, pleased
With himself, the level of his accomplishment,
A studio in a sought-after district in the city.
He was of a certain type urban centers attract,
Street singers whose voices are only passably better
Than the ones that are silent around them on corners,
Whose renditions are not so much heard but witnessed,
As if willingness were the thing that separates
Performers from their audiences. She had not said
She liked his work, but he thought it or did not care.
What mattered to him was how he felt, eyes open
Or shut, he felt good to himself all the same.
Like his presumptive good looks or many silver rings,
Something about him was rough hewn yet buffed,
His long hair a more golden blond than hers,
His blue jeans better fitting. She had been looking
At one of his twilights at sea, bending before
The canvas to catch a closer look at something

That was flotsam or a build-up of paint when she
Caught him through his sunglasses peering down
The line of her blouse, openly and boldly, she thought,
Like a man on deck—not expecting the sun's response.
She colored and frowned. Brightly, he covered
Himself and asked whether she really believed
In the powers of St. Christopher (who hung between
Her breasts like the martyr himself). Off balance,
She began a rambling talk about saints and painters
And dog friends in the country where she had lived
As a girl. She liked the way he focused on her,
Stripping his glasses with an attentive gesture,
Listening and picturing the landscapes she told
The way she might have done them were she the artist.
He was a seasoned veteran of his scene and climate,
Knew that silence and speech were shadow and color,
That young women from the country could be inspired
By white tablecloths and glasses of house wine
As he talked of drifting, sacrifice, and the artist's life.
Later at his place, gathering up her underthings
By the light of the city, she stood at the window
Deciding if she would go. She saw herself both
There and here like the peaks of the roofs outside
And the reflection of him asleep on the bed.
She saw herself in the here and now, a figure
Amid the figures of cathedrals and clock towers,
Bookshelves and kettles, a geometry of dark and light
Like the brindled ancient streets alterable in a moment.

Thin Song of the Leaky Faucet

Drop by drop
Or drip by drip

Each drip or drop
In the open drain

Sounds the note
That cannot hold

Back, builds up
A calculus

On the otherwise
Stainless steel,

Greens the copper
Below the welds,

Returns home
After miles of piping

Reformulated
By minerals

Bacteria
Chemicals

Through the plants
Of power or treatment,

Recongregated
In rivers and wells,

Clouds and seas:
(Each month

The statistics
Of waste inform me

My inabilities
To repair

What should be easy,
How I am

A small but genuine
Exploiter of resources,

Forgetful by day
What I learn each night

Over and again
The similar talk

Of peace and war
Like a spousal nagging)

Each one falling
From a great height

Like a person diving
Out of a circle

Into a circle
The pool of time

That ticks or tocks.

As I Dispose of an Old Encyclopedia

I think of the territories
With their changed names
Like some married women,
Aliases of politics and faith,
The sinuous borders that keep
Cartographers in business,
Undertakers too,
Appellations of deposed monarchs
Or gods no longer relevant;
My grandfather, for instance,
A man I never encountered,
Left his plot in the Ukraine/
Poland/Galicia/Russia,
Understood several languages
(one no longer current),
Could perform activities
Related to the earth,
Chose not to inherit
What was planned for him
(to be laughed at in a boxcar
on the tracks to the future),
Died at an early age
(the disease now curable),
Having altered his name
In New York City
Which has been called many things.

The Door

You shut me out, you let me in,
Like a certain person of my past,
Your angle changes but you remain
Indifferent. With your friends,
Bolt and Key, you permit.
Janus of the threshold, my own
Where I stand to peer through
Your eye, where I speak
In ratty pajamas the voice
Of the tuxedo. I lean against
The cool of your paint,
While you, grained harvest
Of the old-growth forest,
Keep your ancestral calm.
I know others knock your wood,
The dunners of my soul.
You endure etc., unimpresssed,
Gravestone of the hallway,
Lid of the vertical coffin
Where I feign sleep, alive
As I address you. I say
The walls envy your slam,
The panes of windows tremble.
In the surrounding plaster
Worry lines appear.
You shut me out, you let me in,
Strong and simple,
And like joy and sorrow
Hang on the hinge.

A Tenant at Will

I no longer live on Linnaean Street
Where I watched the others going to work
As I drank coffee and smoked a pipe,
Inventing my current existence.
I was not bothered by the phone much.
No credit cards and little to bank.
My typewriter had just gone electric.
Nights I returned after drink and talk
To the punctuation of the white spark
On the trackless trolley wire.
And the slow-moving populace of summer
And the naked sub-lessee
In the lamplight flossing her teeth
Whether I looked or not were there.
Honks and voices and stereo speakers.
Those were the windows of that life.
Some faced a courtyard, the others a street.
I would like to visit who lives there now,
See how my face remains there framed.

Neighbor to What Happens

Once she was married she had to give up
Those clubs she had formerly attended—
Still the nights wore on and more than once
Waking up to see it was before midnight
And he was sleeping in his concentrated manner
Before the next day's surgery—still the need
To party without end, to flirt and dance
In tight clothes, to let the men and women
Admire her posture, timing, and smile,
Rub her a little that they should not know
Her for the good person she is—how much
She loves her family, how she visits patients
In hospices, works at the shelter, walks a greyhound,
Holds degrees in French, poly sci, and counseling,
Still pauses before eating non-union produce,
Has men wear condoms even in her fantasies,
Wants at this moment to be out on the floor,
The wha-wha distorting and strobe dividing
Each figure, when as a girl she wore a dark bra
And white shirt under the purply black lights,
Then bumping hips among mirrors and fog,
And later all in black slamming in the pit,
How she drank then only diet soda, now white
Wine her husband declares legal and cheap;
When once his attraction was his ability
To write prescriptions, now he says things
In near conscious mockery of the tv shows
Her parents thought funny, which makes her
Remember sitting on the floor in front of the couch,

Content and contained, being pet like the family dog,
The pattern of rings on the coffee table
Evidence of their numerous televised dinners—
Her parents' dancing hands upon her back
Like feet making invisible marks on the floor,
The minutes and seconds of every timed song,
A sense of her fleeting well being—like the running
Of the shower and the humming of the fan
While she blows the smoke out the bathroom window.

Poem for Jack

When she and I began sleeping together
Her phone would ring and her answering
Machine click on with your hurt voice leaving
Concerned then clever oaths and messages.
Naked in bed, we laughed at you, and I,
Greedy, held her as she offered me no
Explanation. Before long I was the one
Leaving her the fourth-rung message.
Seeing her at the store after all
This time, she says how well she does,
Catches me up on the news of those
Brief days we spent together, mentions
Your name as if outside her body and mind
We three had met and become old friends.

The Moth

I

More brittle of wing
Than most flying creatures,
With twin tattoos inscribed
On its dusty self, still
Against the window screen
In the morning light
When the house is darker
Than the exterior world
Where I of my habit
Collect the morning paper,
The porch bulb a redundant
Jewel in its copper setting,
Something to be remembered.

II

Once, turned out early
From her basement apartment
By contempt and the necessity
To feed the parking meter,
I walked too many blocks
Of the just risen city,
Where I had found a space
Between the drifts and packed
Vehicles the night before.
There, beside the delivery
Entry of a large hotel
Between two planters filled
With discolored ice and leaves,

Where tulip bulbs were hidden,
A woman slept upon the grating.

III

I had been betrayed!
I saw them through her window,
The way her head tilted back
For his kiss and how her back
Arched when he felt her breasts.
I recall the vision of him:
His shoulder blades through his shirt
As he worked himself against her,
Making her eyes close in
Expressions that meant her pleasure,
And the reasons for not answering
The phone when I called earlier,
An emptiness that summoned me
To the alley where her light burned.

IV

Lying on her stomach, her woolen
Scarf covering half her face,
Stringy dark hair protruding
From the fold of her ski cap,
She clung to the bars
With finger bitten gloves,
Her lumpy body stuffed

Like a filled laundry bag
From all her layers of clothes.
She must have felt protected
In this good part of the city
As the heat rose beneath her
From the generators venting,
Though her back seemed frozen.

V

The moment the buttons opened
The drapes should have closed,
The way in dreams you wake
When things start getting interesting.
From my place against the glass
I willed this go no further
And walked around the corner
And pressed the bell until
She buzzed to let me in.
He passed me on the stairs.
Our favorite wine was open,
The bed itself unstraightened.
A shadow, I lay down
In the light where he had been.

The Squanderers

Hey it's been fourteen years since that summer
We drove the little green Citroën out of Paris
Through Lyon to the blue coast and went Mediterranean,
Wearing no or little clothes, dozing in the bedchairs,
The naked democracy of the beach, appreciating the sun
Who was now making famous European love.

Late afternoon on the tide on my canvas raft,
I drifted out to the moorings and viewed the decks
Of yachts where other men and women toasted
Their good fortune, I supposed. I made the international
Sign of the glass and drank from my hand a draft of air.
Someone said something back I could not understand.

Your body on shore was dark as a ten franc coin.
The bronze gel sank in the ridges of your muscled
Lines, melted and pooled up in your belly.
You heated the lotion, circling it in
The manner I should have applied it there,
As though you were polishing a magic lamp.

What wishes would you give yourself, if from
Your flesh a genie rose to grant you some?
A mother who would live forever, great art,
Recognition, a happy child, a fine house,
Firm breasts, no wrinkles, endless wealth, or like that
Punch line in the old joke, you might have called my name.

Flirt

As if drawn in pencil
The face would be erasable,
Except for the lips and brow,
Those features that suggest
The horizontals of the manner,
How it is the arms are spread
That hints of the bedroom
And seeks its best to hide
The quality of the eyes,
The small imperfect teeth
And ringed blunt fingers.
When I look at the feet
Bare in summer in sandals
I conclude the harsh
Squareness of the toes
Must be a defect of the soul.
She moves in sudden shifts,
Surrounds herself with smoke,
And when her heels scuff back
Below the restaurant table
They strike twin flints
As she laughs and tells us how
Since she went away to school
She gave up wearing underwear.
Oh no, how will we ever stop
Seeing them not there?

An Adult Situation

Of course she should not have found it,
This book she gave him and said to keep
After he moved himself out of her place.
Of course she should not have touched it,
But there it lay beneath the stack
Of mail on his desk, its black cover
Below the white envelopes, the gold
Letters stating exactly what it was.
Of course she should not have parted it
To the place where he had written down
The negative constructions about her,
And the wine and gifts and other details
Of betrayal as bad as the affairs themselves,
Like the one with this apartment's former tenant.
Of course she should not have read it,
The pages of the book like the soiled
Sheets she might have slept on here,
Sheets she bought for him to feel
Close to her, their flannel like her
Nightgown she wore to bed while waiting
For him to touch her. No changing them now!
Of course she should not have left it
Back in the position where he had placed it
With the bills for his phone calls to lovers,
The electricity he used to see them by,
And the heat that would keep them warm.
Of course she should not have done it,
Taken off all her clothes and gone in
To the bathroom where he was showering,
Opened the distorted glass door
Behind which he stood soapy and aroused.

Mine and Not Mine

Once there was mine and what was not mine.

Mine was familiar, passed-on, genetically encoded.
Mine felt good.

Not mine traveled great distances.
Not mine won a race in the rain.

I gave up mine for what was not mine.

A Mass Hallucination of Motels

Say that it's not you driving from Las Cruces
To Santa Rosa, or that it's nobody but you
At the wheel, your hands at two and ten
O'clock the way your father taught years ago
After work at the store he called the place.
Beside you on the bench seat he narrated
The streets of little beach towns in off
Season sleep, which intersections were
Most dangerous. True enough, there'd been
Wrecks, the signs ignored or newly posted.
Holding on to the absent wheel, he dropped
His shoulder, turned the corners with you,
His right foot pressing to accelerate,
His right foot readying to brake. He was,
You recall, a dealer of furniture. In
His shirt and tie he loaded his own trucks.

I know that it's you driving from Santa Rosa
To Amarillo, the sun like a high beam
In the rearview mirror, when the song comes
On the radio like a pre-programmed miracle
Amid the grim preaching and interference.
The theme song of your life when you were
The main character, and the film rolls out
On the reel of the road where billboards
For food and fuel, fireworks and casinos
Paint vague sensations of pleasure and danger
Awaiting your exit, the ever so often crawl
Of the same motels under the deepening sky.

Maybe this could be your next great season,
You as yourself at night on a highway in summer,
The world a wheel, the wheel analogic,
Your each setting forth a heading home.

The Art of the Possible

Here is a place you may have been,
Childhood furnishings, pennants and posters
Of what you admired, favored
Of the gods, born in the gold painted
Room where the sea outside your windows
Schooled you in the waves' persistence,
Where gulls in upward drafts taught
A purposeful ease by which you are not known.

And here are the kind parents who stand round
Your fever bed or the little bad dream
That brings them to you across the green
Carpet thick in air conditioned rooms.
Loving son, your role: to see again
Patterns of light on the ceiling and wall,
The look of things as they disappear,
Sea spray lit in the air.

The Restaurant by the Pier

I

Lipstick rubbed off a water glass,
Fingerprints washed from silverware,
Little evidence of the would-be diners
Lined-up among shadows at the door,
Waiting as the old school taught
While the first course of crustaceans
Steamed like a navy in broth.

II

Dressed in blue shirts and white caps,
Deck shoes and the relevant insignia
They were the summer people then, seen
By the staff as the wine they ordered,
The time or two they sent back a dish,
Asked for butter, water, or rolls,
Inquired about a possible menu to go.

III

Out of season, behind iced windows
Mobiles of flounder, swordfish, and cod
Swim through the air, a current of light;
And there upon the dust frosted bar,
The boss inventories his measured stock.
Rap at the glass. He will let us in.
But he's a fabric walrus. Nothing's on his floe.

Without People

Fault the young
        squirrel
                for not being
On the red oak
        branch
                where the ivy stops
And the sun
        begins,
                his place in the morning
Light vacant,
        a sign
                like those recollected
Winter beach
        motels,
                their lots and rooms
With beds awaiting
        the mind
                populates its cities
Towns, suburbs and
        land-
                scapes of forest,
Mountain, and shore—
        what is
                known by one
Now seen by all
        the gull
                of childhood perches
On the wooden frame
        that holds
                the boat and written rules

On the lifeguard stand
        inform forever
                no ball playing,
Picnic lunches, or
        radios
                allowed, for this
Is an orderly
        place
                beside an inhuman sea.

Dweller

The evidence held that I was a limited person
So I walked out among thickets and hills
To a place where the ancients left their mark,
A bluff where the city appeared a distant cluster,
Its storied inhabitants frivolously troubled.

—Hmm, transit and the foibles of the heart.
A man and a woman lie down in a field
And where they sleep a settlement begins.
Vegetables grow through the grasses.
Animals step from the woods to be changed.

The Elevation

A man awake early watches for the sunrise.
He is sure of this, a given thing
He has seen between ranges and out of the sea.
From boyhood to fatherhood it's been the same.
Strange to find a constant in a moving thing.
Strange to think it strange and to say so at dawn.

(In her parents' bed, she nurses one breast and tugs at the other.
Such a comfort to know another always there—
Like Father on the patio before leaving for work,
And the faith through the long day that he will come home.)

Basho, Buson, Issa, Greensboro

My new dog in the garden barking

Late December finds me in shirtsleeves

Sun like a pat of melted butter in the white sky

Sun all morning in rising

The squirrel is world's champion tightrope walker

Woodpeckers in the old maple seem likely

I picture myself well in the chair where I'm not yet sitting

The branch shaking the garden gate who's there

Certain limbs hold dead twigs must have an explanation

Reason is the wind has not found them out

Although they are bare and beautiful I do not sleep with the trees

Another day in the leaves

Wind on the Moon

There was a roaring in the mind last night,
A child's fever about the house. Cold
Cloths were brought, the thermometer shaken.
Now the morning light has given back
To the dogwood trees their celery color,
And the sun has buttered the walls of our house.

*

My daughter on my hip
Like a figurehead
On the prow of a ship
Sailing sideways
Through the Mediterranean
Light of the kitchen,
Where a bowl of lemons
Suggests tropical islands,
Orchids on the sill
A mountainous jungle.

The shelved assembly
Of crockery stares
Like gods of antiquity
On the cliff unblinking.
We cruise the blue tile
To a Gibraltar of stove,
Where fish beached
In flour and basil
Swim in the tide
Of bubbling oil.

*

The reel takes a long time to unwind
Its question mark back into the sea.
Surf-fishing in my waders in the waves,
I lose the hook in the gold of the sun.

I feel the weight sink through the wind.
The fish may not answer today—but see
People on the shore who look like me wave.
They are my parents and I am still a son.

Full Circle

It is frustrating not to know things,
To have no word for purple or fox,
That Florida and France are different places,
And walking in the rain stops being fun.

The sea is sometimes not always the ocean.
Salt and sugar have fooled others.
No matter how many times you ask him,
The cat will never read you a book.

Words for Arborists

Contrary wind
        that split
                the front yard
Maple
        I worked to strip
                of clinging ivy
The ghost of which
        lines the bark
                in hieroglyphs
To spell forever
        in words of arborists
                that life of branches;

Woodsman your axe
        has swooned the summer
                shade of a friend
To our house
        a canopy recalled
                absent in the heat
Of curtained windows
        upstairs and down.
                If once on the lawn I relaxed
Don't take what I try
        too late to protect,
                birds astonished wheeling.

Crooked Wood

Here in the brighter yard, cleared of brittle
And split branches, I tend my patch of lawn,
Inscribed *sharply now by the trees' calligraphy,*
The linear and curlicued, altered suggestion
Of the root work under the soil, the ropes
And threads that tie the yard together, a binding
Contract of earth and wood, my little piece
Of what was forest, wilder now below the surface

As yet unpaved. Although I love this place,
Chair in full sun in the morning, the long
Light at the end of the day that in December
Keeps my legs in shorts, my arms in short sleeves,
It's sidewalks up north I miss, their constant
Human message, the sharp heel sounds
On hurried people, the flat stamp of work
Boots on just cleared pavement, by the snowbank

Steam rising from the coffee and exhalations
Of workers on break around a manhole cover,
The abbreviated utilities scribbled in Dig Safe.
And what of that remembered anticipation
Going in a shop or bar, the temporary, important
Moment before the choice of an aisle or chair
When all eyes for an instant are upon you,
When your eyes seek out no match or mirror

But the oblivion of an object found, the ringing
Of the register. It's true I slept later then.

(Why does one wake early with nothing to do?)
And sometimes with my arms around someone
I proposed breakfast to her outside the apartment—
For nothing we wanted could be made of out-of-date
Milk, collected mustards, and take-out containers
From the Indian, Thai, and Chinese restaurants

Cohabiting the chill of my undefrosted refrigerator.
Hand in hand we walked to our heaven,
The greasy spoon down the block where other
Couples also dressed in last night's clothes.
Who were we then? A couple of warm ones
Under some blankets, two piles of black clothes
On a hardwood floor. Those plaster walls
Of the brownstones would not need mending.

Word comes south of a friend's death
By natural causes, meaning no one can say
What it is that so exactly fails us,
Heart or head or the veins of circulation.
I recall the crisp angles his shirt made,
His arms expressively bent through the vest
As he leaned forward to grab his whisky glass
And laughed too loudly whatever the joke.

In my trees Jeff and Jon from Crooked Wood
Have trimmed the post oak and the maple
Then hauled the truckloads to the country
Where their friends will gather around a bonfire

Of kindling branches and lengths of seasoned trunks.
A father of young children and a son of old ways,
I knock the wood of the trees that stand in my yard
Like coatless men in the simplest of drawings.

For George V. Higgins

The Puppet's Complaint

You never raise my arms anymore,
Old performer, sacked in the sheets,
Your eyes enclosed by the white curtain
Of brows and beard, come back tired
From your job as watchman at the brewery.

Leaning at the angle you left me in,
Against the chill of the dresser mirror,
I watch to see if you are really breathing,
Propped in bed so late in the morning.
The flowerless coverlet stained.

The lace from your marriage spreads tattered
On the nightstand beneath the cup of teeth.
On the walls hang pictures in their frames,
Posters and playbills of the lost theaters,
Dark for years, then torn away.

My strings are twisted and frayed. Alone
At night on your rounds do you think
How once we dressed alike, how still
I wear that suit, those gloves of felt.
But it's the shoe box for me, I'm afraid.

I have seen how you look in the new costume
The way it fits you ill at wrist and waist,
How it makes you half your size and all
Your age: it waits on the back of the door,
Another puppet expecting you to wake.

The Hundred Pieces

"I was afraid the plane would be late
And I thought of me up there in your seat,
How much I would fidget and twist the skin
On the back of my hand. And I thought
I should have paid your first class fare,
That you deserved one for having come so far
In answering me with yourself in the flesh.
It is good to see you and hold you close,
To embrace as we do. Your eyes are clear
And your color is good. Something has been
Always vital in you, a veneer of health
Like the skin of a gorgeous apple. I hope
Your mother is well and your father has begun
To feed himself again. I have these Edenic
Memories of them, your mother carving
The roast, swimming in her element, your father
Miraculously switching from scotch to gin.
Sometimes during grandiose imaginings
Of my death, I pretend I am being devoured
There in the bosom with a good cabernet,
Your family remarking on the qualities
I have brought to the sauce. Don't look that way.
The line for the toll is always a bore, watching
The solitary drivers or the anxious passengers
Waiting for the brief moment of their greeting,
The payment, the bell, the rising of the gate.
Then on to the city that now seems worth it.
I see that you have brought me a gift. I will wait
To open it later, perhaps after you leave

It will tell me how I should have received you,
Whether it will sit on the mantel like a reproach.
I have fixed you up a corner of my living room
And placed a chair in good light near the window
Where you can read or watch the workers
Taking down the building across the street.
I know that low level of distraction you enjoy.
I think we will be able to get our work done
And I will give you what privacy I have.
There is a person who visits me sometimes
When the bars close. I lie back on the white rock
Of my bed, my hands behind my neck as if bound.
My angel is an eagle with the face of leather,
An idea that engenders from my classical education
And the study I have made of personal advertisements.
In my library is a picture of the drawn and quartered,
The handsome limbs stacked like cordwood.
It is called *The Hundred Pieces* and each time I look
I find one more thing, but never have I been able
To reach that numerical perfection, the exact
Total unaccountable, just as how I have failed
To reason how the body stays alive through each
Subtraction, yet through it all seems to the observer
The head on its post of spine appears to be smiling.
Like the way you must feel after a day of traveling,
Leaving a little of yourself here and there as folks do?"

Confession of a Ghost

Even then he was in some ways invisible,
At the wheel, anonymous as the passing cars,
The people inside them chatting nice things
When he came out of nowhere, out of control,
In a late model vehicle, on the wrong side
Of the road, in the twilight, a certain shift
In a lane he should have known, having driven
This route half a million times. A tragic
Mistake in judgment brought on by exhaustion,
And something he had had a little earlier
In the day, after having received a little bad
News at work where he had said something
Under his breath, a habit he was known for
By his children and wife, they having waited
Long enough for the changes he promised
Half a million times. He was figuring
Nearly a hundred himself and was in between
Not caring enough about one thing and another
When the van appeared just in front of him,
Its driver wore a moustache, was smoking
When the doors popped open upon impact
And out flew the children sleeping on laps,
And parents, cousins, uncles, aunts flying
In their traveling clothes, some through glass,
Like performers caught without a net.
He never felt more human until their death.

Imperfections of the Skin

On a block near the river was a small shop
She wanted to step into, but never could
She venture beyond the glass or threshold
Where the posted bills and color circulars
Promoted various local activities—
Tattoos, piercings, intermediate covens,
Bands performing in warehouse clubs,
Workshops for magicians, and candle making.
A man who worked there troubled her,
Who came to the window when she paused
Outside by the racks of books and incense
In her tennis clothes or when she came by
Wheeling the stroller. It was not the little boy
He seemed to be after. Each time he watched
Her through the glass as if it were his right.
Since a child herself, she had been studied by men,
But he was not admiring her lengths and curves.
He seemed to appraise the surface of her flesh,
As his eyes took in larger pores and wrinkled places,
Little breakouts, and the scars apparent on her chin
From an accident at ten. She would shiver and retreat,
Only to return later in the week when again
He would appear, his bald or shaven skull
Placed as if it belonged among the sculptures
And antique weaponry displayed in the window.
His age was uncertain. He had flat blue eyes.
For the rest of him she imagined a black or white
Collarless shirt, loose-fitting trousers, rope sandals.
He is not from around here, she would think,

A thing people back home said about people—
But she was not from around here either.
A young grandmother, she was visiting her daughter
Who had no husband but a child and several boyfriends.
She was trying to be useful and stay out of the way.
One afternoon walking without the baby she browsed
Outside the shop when he came through the door.
He was taller than she pictured yet wore the outfit
She chose in her mind for him. She wanted to run
When he raised a hand for her to stay in place
And she was moving ever so slightly when he said,
"I have a lotion that might be useful to you
Made of ground silk, certain flowers, and the milk
Of a tree found only in equatorial Asia.
Would you like me to apply the first treatment?"
Later in the apartment after the child and her daughter
Were asleep and after her shower, she took
A long look at herself in the magnifying mirror.
She regretted that she had not taken the clay jar
He had offered or at least read the scrawl of the label.
On another day she was tired, having pushed
The stroller uphill and down and gone to several
Stores, and the little one was finally napping,
When she stopped outside the shop and sat on the steps
Until he appeared. His voice was quiet and slow
As if the sum of his presence had worn away
All of her previous vigilance and caution.
After all he was the only person in the city
Who gave her any kind of acknowledgment.

She was comforted when again he said,
"I have a lotion that might be useful to you
Made of ground silk, certain flowers, and the milk
Of a tree found only in equatorial Asia.
Would you like me to apply the first treatment?"
She shook her head but he implored her anyway
To take the jar he said "for free," showing her
In small circular motions in the air how it was
He said the lotion must be applied so that the skin
Might drink and heal. It rained the next day
And she did not wish to go out. The child
Played at day care and her daughter was at her job.
In the quiet apartment after her shower,
She put on a little music and spread a bath sheet
Over the sofa and opened the jar he had given her
Whose label was not handwritten words but a drawing
Of a mountain and several figures in the foreground.
The lotion was blue and scented of many flowers—
Rose, jasmine, hyacinth, gardenia?—
But no one fragrance isolated. She touched
Her fingers to its surface which felt grainy
And a little resistant. It seemed harmless
When she rubbed a dab on the back of her arm
Then across her chest and torso using both hands.
On her face it felt both warm and cool, the scent
So heavy she felt a little dizzy but it did not burn
As she had feared. She rubbed it into the scars
Of her forehead and the lines around her eyes
In ever smaller circles as she remembered his hands'

Instruction in smaller and smaller circles
And soon she was asleep in the meadow
Where herons watched the motion of her breath
And the distant mountains were those on the label.
Waking suddenly to the sound of her own name
And the cry of a baby, she saw the figure of her daughter
Standing above her, looking at her body on the sofa
As if she had become a skeleton, that the lotion
Removed the skin from her pile of bones—but no,
It was merely the terrible recognition of a daughter
Shocked at seeing a mother naked on the sofa,
The music having switched from jazz to klezmer
Before the daughter's appearance, the damp towel
Beneath the mother when the daughter said, "Mother,"
The fancy jar within reach on the cocktail table.

Stevedore

In a different time, in a different body,
In a different life, in a different city,
With different eyes, with different clothing,
With a different voice, with a different bearing,
I might have been a laborer in some tropical
        port of call,

Where I would work long hours in the sun
That beat as it burned in permanent noon,
Reflecting its gift of coins on the water
For harbor children who would dive there
Only to surface with the slime from the bottom
        clutching a button.

Where is the gold that has turned to brass?
In some sea trunk in the tidal trough.
On board the captain glares through the porthole.
I think of him tonight when I buy my bottle
Along the docks where I ask my question—
        the hook in my hand.

A Traveler

Not a pleasure
Seeker exactly,
If measured
By the diagonal
Lines of the forehead
Possibly mistaken
For the seams of a ball
Or the index of the bear
Market; face brushed
With a common condition
Of liquor and the skin;
A nose in the light
Unkind to his prospects;
The nearly sympathetic
Eyes moist as a dog's;
Dry but kissable lips;
Well-spaced teeth;
Chin blunt and wanting;
Not a body
Builder exactly,
More a part loser;
Various organs
Taken by disease;
Brain hurt and hurt heart;
Not a good dancer,
Arms locked around
Someone walking backwards.

Prague

Of stone, quarried
In the mind from
Riverbanks
And deep places
Of earth where
Bronze tips
Lodged in decayed
Chests of vanished
Creatures, city
Of workhorses
And alchemists,
Palaces and back
Alleys, jumble
Of language, pressure
Point of sovereignty,
Place I have never
Seen but where
My old ones
Walked for a thousand
Years, knuckle
On the hand of Europe,
Signature of the arrest
Warrant at the station.

Acts of Love

These heroic days of summer
Warding off boredom with gin
And tonic and a magazine

Long legs across the bones
Of an Adirondack ottoman
Catalogue item 2b

Ordered assembled and delivered
With the chair on whose blue arms
Rests the drink, the article

That concerns the person much
Like the person you once made
Of yourself attired and afoot

In a strange and foreign city
Alone as was your custom then
When the play was in your head

And the dialogue was lively
And people wondered if you were
Available for acts of love.

Chorus of the Horses

We on the carpet, the meadow,
At the edge of the fruit trees
Where the field starts listen
To hear the slowing pattern
Of the hoofs on the path at night
Of one who holds her every note
Or sigh, her every neigh
Through arched, gated walls
On the road from the capital
To tell us what we fear,
New men on the ramparts,
The old king gone, the search
For his children escaped on the mare.

The Fisherman and the Dryad

He drank from a bottle and waded in the river.
He waded near the bank and watched the light
Drain through the trees and set on the water
That told his fortune with floating sticks and leaves.
He saw his place arranged there before him,
A dinner service set on a table of glass
That he, the thrown rock of himself, might break,
His own reflection, the gray shadow of a fish,
Its murky back twisting through stumps and weeds.

Then he heard her step through the forest, the sound
Of the steps preceding her through the leaves
Like the calling card of a doe approaching the water,
Trying her footing across newly covered ground.
Back packer, he thought, and put away his bottle,
Not wanting it a stranger's first sight of him,
Cheered it could be someone who liked a line of chatter,
He, not having spoken to anything but a worm
All day in the forest instead of at work.

He had been changing a flat, a roofing nail
Pried from the tread with the edge of a dime,
Rolling the spare when he first heard the river
On the other side of the road when his breathing slowed.
Having heard it, he wanted to see it at once,
To wade in his boots and drag a cast line
In the flat current moving toward him,
When she stepped into the clearing above the river,
Stripping bark from her arms, brushing birds from her hair.

The Landscape Artist

Like this: the broad stripe of the road
Through the fragrant countryside,
The white sky blue at its edges,
The sea beyond the low, silver rail
Green toward the black of deep water,
And somewhere inside the tree line,
Depending how far you are willing to go,
Deer in the leaves like lovers dressing
Vanish when you hoped you would surprise them.

From your place at the easel, like a pilgrim
You wore your shoe leather through the sole,
A distant tower seen across a farmed valley,
Its bells of arrival sounding in your ears,
A harvest horn for the solitary traveler
Returned to a place where he never lived,
Where relatives dote upon newfound darlings,
Where the living are too present to bear,
And everything means more than it should.

Stone in my heel crept in. Entering
Among scrub pine and aloe, I have been
Trying to make something happen, picture
You within the scene then step back
To look over your canvas as if from a flight deck
Or as a face on a ship might tell the shore
From a flat place on the water after a storm.
This landscape says you were not afraid yet
Of what started painting shut the corners of your eyes.

Half Himself

I

In sunlight beside a dry November pool,
The vinyl-slatted outdoor furniture
Left impressions in the pastel linen
Of his out of season suit. From his perch
He appraised the tiled roofs and the wakes
Of container vessels ploughing the sea
Beyond the harbor. Was it really November?
The morning heat undignified as an August
Noon, little pearls of coffee sweat clung
To the lip of his cup. Last night a kiss,
Her tongue like a duchess in salon among
The collected statuary, went no further.
His vow was old as the knights he drew
On napkins and memoranda. Another face
Had been his grail. He had had his chance,
The choosing done, questions poorly answered.
His heart was an empty bed; his body
The sole hotel guest. His room was waiting
Above the veranda, its window affording
The bellman and maid the fine view of him.

II

But who was he to be seen as such?
A so-and-so no longer up-and-up,
Exile to the inappropriate month,
His topcoat on the chairback hung
Like the director's of another era

Of wide lapels and the teeming pool
And the band playing a foreign strain
For the Bacchus of the course
And the willows in their shorts
Sipping brightly colored drinks
In the closing fire of the sun;
Time for the credits in the large font
To see who played whom and never skip
Those happy names that spring to health
From the deepest lake or vein-fed well,
A fountain to the arid land,
Otherwise an insubstantial self,
The image of a character of film
Projected in the out of doors
Over brickwork and molding.

III

Someone's air force is leaving
Vapor trails in the cerulean sky,
And someone's enterprise is hauling
Letters above the shoreline,
Avowals of love in bold caps,
Mile high promotions for local
Eating and drinking establishments.
Goodbye to the world of slow recognition.
Hello to the news of the too-close plane,
A reminder of the industrial machinery
That is always grinding somewhere,
Like the drone of a distant lecture

When he was a student of someone,
And the body of knowledge was near
As a classmate guiding his hands.
Something was imminent then,
Like a figure stepping out of its clothes,
Like a figure climbing out of the pool
Rung by rung up the steel ladder.

IV

He wrote a letter on the hotel stationery,
Its salutation in a clear, broad hand.
The *dear* seemed intimate though forced.
Already he detected the problem of tone.
Folding it over he wanted it right
Like the cleft in a Windsor knot.
The water's solution proved reflective.
He prefaced the *dear* with *my*,
Attaining a little of the personal
Yet brusque in his mannered way,
This peculiar state he was heir to,
Monarch of transparency, born
To the confiscated lands, whose dear
Deposed heads acquired their fame
For squandering familial misfortune.
He would accept the generous offer
Of her car and driver. He would pay
The anticipated visit. The management
Had made all the necessary arrangements.
Comb, toothbrush, and razor in his pocket.

Marina Azul

You come here with a beat-up suitcase,
Half a dozen books, and a map
With more creases than roads. Although
You do not walk you are covered with dust,
Having followed the rail line to the sea.
Marina Azul. You are welcome here,
Says the station master who knows
The language you still speak. Here
Is the bay to swim in, and the shabby
Boats look jaunty at their distance.
You think of all you have left behind
And it does not seem like much,
Think of someone you might tell this
But there are no phones in Marina Azul
And you have abandoned the practice of postcards.
In your hotel room above the bar,
Stains on the bedspread, coffee or blood.
The notion that others have slept here before you
No longer troubles you, though the seal
On the water bottle is cracked and the glasses
Beside it smell like wine. Late in the night,
The songs from below keep you awake
As you sit on the little porch, chair tipped
Against the shutters, bare feet upon the rail.
Youth has left you and now all of age.
Marina Azul, you have finally arrived,
A village from childhood invented on a map.

From the Anthology of Dreams of Death: Harlequin Dream

I walked the streets without a guidebook,
Passed photographs of the naked
Advertising soap or telephone sex.
I had the urge to press my chest
Against someone's chest
But settled for the air instead,
Improving my posture as I went,
A thread of hair from the back of my head
Adjusting my skeleton.
You were lurking behind some bend
In the structure. I had to follow,
Circling the Winter Circus in the rain.

From the Anthology of Dreams of Death: Maritime Dream

What it was like to be naked
In a tub with the water
On the outside did not
Look so odd to me then
Until the sun rose, leaving
Me more apparent to myself;
The unclipped nails at the ends
Of my toes curled, and above
The prow where the faucet should have been
Stood the outlying lengths of the splintery piers
And the old hotels of a vanished sky.

From the Anthology of Dreams of Death:
Aerial Dream

I flew in a wooden plane to California.
My seat was not assigned. I stalled
Among the rows of passengers,
A young woman in a velvet hat
I recognized by the window,
A pair of well-dressed men I took to be lawyers,
A pilot returning to his hub,
Ruffians in tee shirts smoking by the toilets.
We rode through pockets and blue spaces.
I shifted my weight and saw that I was barefoot,
At last a surfer of the clouds.

The Figure

Clouds rose up to my high heaven
And from my aerie purchase
I spied the brown rat
In pursuit of cover. The sun I knew
Had not yet set. Dry leaves
Spun in the treetops.
People shook their heads in fear
Of weather. From many hands
Umbrellas sprouted, as the hailed
Cabs passed richly passengered.
Merchant and barber, client and customer,
All the patients of physicians,
Psychiatrists, opticians
Left table, couch, or consulting chair,
And out through the doorway
Into the expected sunlight
As if at the news of assassination.
The avenues resembled public highways.
Families crossed like wary raccoons.
At intersections headlights were eclipsed
By walkers holding bundles and valises.
Baggy shadows engaged in motion.
No handclasps or horseplay, only the muted
Urgency of the swiftly moving river.

Then it was that I descended
In the garb of my accustomed manner,
The dark suit of the future laundered,
Trousers all fresh creases;

The black tie of history slipped from my neck;
Having endured boredom, the Great Terror,
The Romans, the Christians, the Nazis, etc.,
And the highly personal bang in the chest,
I revisited the alleyways and mazes
Of the old city, the cafes and cages
Where the slaughterhouse piano plays
Tunes for human curiosities;
Hard not to picture the renderings of demons,
The rapture and knowledge of beak and jaw
As they eat, still warm, the heart;
So it was time that I surrendered
Disheveled, discounted, driven
To every treason; funny
As the X-ray of a clown,
Under my feathers I am light as bone.

BIOGRAPHICAL NOTE

Stuart Dischell is the author of *Good Hope Road* and *Evenings &
Avenues*. His poetry has won awards from the National Poetry
Series, the National Endowment for the Arts, the North Carolina
Arts Council, and the Pushcart Prize. He teaches in the Program
in Creative Writing at the University of North Carolina at
Greensboro.

Penguin Poets